MW01115779

THE CONDO BOARD SURVIVAL GUIDE

HOW TO KEEP YOUR OWNERS INFORMED AND HAPPY
GET WORK COMPLETED ON TIME
AND SPEND LESS TIME IN BOARD MEETINGS

By

RAFAL DYRDA

Rafal Dyrda
507, 10909 103 Avenue NW
Edmonton AB T5K 2W7
Canada

www.CondoBoardBook.com

The author has worked diligently to provide accurate advice on the topics covered in this book. However, this book is sold with the understanding that the author is not engaged in giving any financial, accounting, legal, or any other professional advice. The author strongly urges anyone who believes they are in need of such advice to seek the services of a qualified professional in their jurisdiction.

Edited By — Sally Wolfe
http://www.bookmanifesto.com/

The Condo Survival Guide/Rafal Dyrda

ISBN-13: 978-1545488539
ISBN-10: 1545488533

BEFORE YOU START READING DOWNLOAD YOUR TOOKLIT FOR <u>FREE</u>!

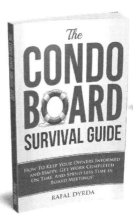

READ THIS FIRST

Just to say thanks for reading my book, I would like to give you a few bonuses to help you on your journey!

Download your **Condo Board Survival Toolkit** by visiting the website below:

www.CondoBoardBook.com/toolkit

Register your book & get your FREE bonuses

Dedication

*I would like to dedicate this book
to my wife, Kinga.*

*Without your support, understanding, and love
I wouldn't be where I am today.
You have changed me as a person,
a husband, and a human being.*

*This book wouldn't exist if you didn't believe in me,
my dreams, and all my crazy ideas.*

Love you always!

Acknowledgments

To all clients and condominium owners.

Thank you for sharing your stories, problems, experiences,
feedback, and suggestion.
It was my pleasure to get to know all of you over
the phone, e-mail, Skype, and chats.
Without your guidance, many of the chapters
in this book wouldn't exist.
I'm always happy to hear from you.

*To family, friends,
and all that shared their advice and ideas.*

Thank you.

TABLE OF CONTENTS

INTRODUCTION

THE REASON FOR THIS BOOK

On November 30th, 2003 my wife and I received the keys to our first property. A two bedroom condominium located in the heart of downtown Edmonton. It was all we wanted and more. Life was wonderful.

Then problems started popping up. The garage door didn't open on our way to work. The elevator didn't function for days on end. The alarm panel in the lobby kept beeping for no apparent reason. And some days the hot water wasn't much warmer than the cold water.

We let things slide. After all, we thought, this was just condo living.

We coasted like this for about two years. Then one day, we came home to a flooded storage room. We had no idea who to contact. The information in the documents we'd been given when we moved in was outdated. Our neighbors were as clueless as we were.

The next day by a miracle I bumped into the president of the board while he was doing maintenance work around the property. He gave me the name and phone number of the property management company. I called and left numerous voicemails. After two days, I finally got a response and spoke to someone who was able to get the repairs moving. But it felt like an eternity.

Eventually, the problem was fixed. A similar story occurred when we needed to get our door buzzer reprogrammed. For six months, we had to run down the stairs to let our visitors in.

Finally, I decided to do something. I went to the Annual General Meeting (AGM) to air my concerns. It wasn't my expectation to join the board. I just wanted for things to be taken care of. To my surprise, someone nominated me. I accepted and was elected president without knowing anything about condominiums. But like you, I wanted to change and improve things. I wanted to help myself and other owners get their issues resolved. I was determined to make a difference. It couldn't be that hard, right?

WAKE-UP CALL

My first board meeting—which lasted 3 hours!—was a huge shock. I quickly discovered there were no efficient processes to handle routine or even urgent problems. The board reviewed requests and letters from residents at the meeting and another month passed before they decided what was going to be done. What was worse, they had no system for keeping track of repairs or requests.

At that time I had my own consulting business in custom software development. I worked with the government, consulting companies and corporations to provide solutions to their problems. It was my passion and what I loved to do. My business had processes in place, people with the right skills and knowledge to do their job. It was a well-oiled machine. This is what I had expected from our condominium board.

YOUR BOARD IS A BUSINESS

I started putting in a lot of hours to get the job done. Volunteer hours I was not being paid for. Much of the time I felt like I was pushing a broken cart down a rutted road. Soon I realized that our board needed a tool to improve communication with the management and the owners, to give people better access to information, and encourage collaboration.

You see, the board was running a six hundred thousand dollar corporation, even though they didn't think of it that way. It might not be a for-profit business, but it was a business nonetheless. A business that was responsible to the shareholders, the owners.

The board you serve on is no different. You have employees to manage. Condominium fees need to be collected. You have to work with the property manager and deal with service providers and vendors. Send out alerts, update documents. You are called upon to make numerous and often difficult decisions. For it to work, you need knowledge and support.

THE NEXT STEP

Between running the condo board and my own consulting business, I soon had no time for a personal life. Something had to give. One weekend I locked myself in my office and **created a solution.** I designed a system to handle all the tasks and processes we needed to accomplish every month. Life got easier.

In 2010, I jumped in with both feet. I closed down my consulting business and started helping condominiums run efficient and cost-effective boards as a full-time venture. Boards that serve residents and keep owners happy. In 2011, I was appointed to the Board of Directors of the Canadian Condominium Institute in North Alberta, Canada. In 2016 I was nominated as The Chairperson of the National Communications Committee.

To this day I'm still a board member at our condominium which I enjoy. Currently, everything is running smoothly. We have a great management company, which provides a fantastic service to our condo and to the entire industry. Our meetings are short and to the point.

WHAT YOU WILL LEARN HERE

All Condo Board Directors want to do their best, but not all know how to make it happen.

Chances are, like me, when you joined your condominium board you had no idea what was involved. You might have started out as a disgruntled or enthusiastic owner but soon got overwhelmed with lengthy meetings and endless back-and-forth emails and phone calls. It doesn't have to be that way. *Becoming a condominium board director can be a rewarding experience.*

If you are ready to become a happy and stress-free board member while making a satisfying and meaningful contribution to your condominium, then this book is for you.

Learn how to:

1. Run your condo board like a business
2. Understand your role as a board member
3. Have short, successful meetings
4. Manage and track work requests with ease
5. Keep your owners informed and happy
6. Create procedures and policies that work
7. Create a strong and supportive community that helps each other.

Once you understand the fundamentals of running your board and put effective processes and tools in place, you will no longer have to spend countless hours trying to keep up with the complaints and tasks that seem never ending.

So let's get started.

CHAPTER 1

WHAT'S A CONDOMINIUM BOARD FOR?

When you first thought about joining your condo board, you probably had one overpowering motivation. You wanted to improve or change the way things were getting done (or were *not* getting done) in your condo.

Maybe you thought the landscaping was looking shabby. Or were embarrassed by the carpet in the lobby area. Perhaps you were tired of the elevator breaking down. Or frustrated that it took several days for the property manager to send out a plumber when you called? You figured if you were on the inside, you could change things. (Oh yeah, and maybe get some answers about the increase in those condo fees.)

Most owners decide to join their condo board because they want to:

- ✔ Get their grievances heard and resolved.
- ✔ Understand how the condo is run and help it run better.
- ✔ Exercise their rights as a condo owner.
- ✔ Stop feeling at the mercy of the property management company.
- ✔ Have a say in how decisions are made.
- ✔ Make the condo a better place to live.

WHAT YOU DIDN'T EXPECT

Whatever your reason, you were probably surprised if you discovered that:

- ✔ Meetings were long (up to 3 hours or more) and poorly run

- ✔ Agendas were unclear
- ✔ Important action items got pushed aside
- ✔ Conflicting opinions and arguments predominated.
- ✔ Some board directors were only concerned with their self-interest.

Still, you were serious. You wanted to make a difference so you took on the tasks that were asked of you, and you got your hands dirty. You were willing to pick up garbage, issue fines, contact owners to collect condo fees, and even paint walls.

WHAT THE BOARD'S RESPONSIBILITIES ARE NOT

There's a problem with this picture.

You see, it's not the board's responsibility to be the janitor, the collections agent, or the contractor. The board's job is to set policies, provide oversight, and ensure that the board itself—owners, residents, and directors—are following the rules and regulations set forth in the acts, bylaws, and policy documents of the Condominium Corporation. (You know, the pile of documents you got when you bought the place.)

In other words, the purpose of the condo board is to run the business of the condominium. And the goal of that business is *to serve the best interest of the owners*. Think of owners as shareholders in a company. If the owners are not happy with the decisions made by the board or how things are run, the board must answer to the owners at the next Annual General Meeting or when a Special Meeting when called.

If your goal is to become a productive and happy member of your board (and I assume it is), you need to know how it functions *as a business*. First and foremost, the board is the legal representation of its owners. Like board members who run any corporation, profit or non-profit, they—meaning you—are the *Decision Makers* and these decisions are binding.

However, before you can make good decisions you need to be aware of the duties and responsibilities of the board. Without this knowledge, you may find your task list growing with every meeting.

PRIMARY FUNCTIONS OF THE CONDO BOARD

Like any board, the board of directors is made up of the usual suspects: president, vice-presidents, treasurer, secretary, and a designated chairperson. Depending on the size of your board, other directors are usually assigned to support and assist these primary roles.

Under the leadership of the president, these are the main functions of the board. (For a detailed list of duties and responsibilities for each position, refer to the Appendix at the end of the book.)

- ✔ Maintain all common property of the condominium and protect the value of owners' real estate.
- ✔ Follow and enforce all condominium acts, regulations, bylaws, and policies.
- ✔ Hire and manage all employees and contractors, such as the Property Manager, Attorney or Accountant.
- ✔ Maintain and review accurate financial records and bank accounts.
- ✔ Review and issue payments for all services.
- ✔ Hold regular board meetings, including the Annual General Meeting or Special General Meeting.
- ✔ Respond to all owner inquiries in a timely fashion.
- ✔ Record and distribute the board minutes to all owners.
- ✔ Create and distribute documents, such bylaws, newsletters, announcement and repair alerts.
- ✔ Collect all condominium fees from owners.
- ✔ Create a monthly financial report and annual budget.
- ✔ Prepare and file taxes if required by rules or bylaws.

WHO'S IN CHARGE?

Sometimes boards turn too many responsibilities over to the condo management company. When that happens roles get reversed and the board ends up taking direction from the condo manager instead of taking the lead. These were the cards dealt me when I joined the board. Our board depended too much on our property manager to "take care of things". Work wasn't completed on time, proper vendors weren't hired, and too many agenda items were tabled over and over until the next meeting, all subject to decisions or actions of the condo manager.

Unfortunately, this is not an uncommon situation. The board, believing they are being efficient, will often give free reign to the condo manager, allowing them to respond to owners, including what actions to take and which vendors to hire. They may authorize the condo manager to sign checks and pay contractors, even invest corporation funds, all without review or approval of the board.

Since it is the board who is responsible for the decisions that are made, not the condo manager, it's essential that board members be involved in the decision-making process as well as be aware of day-to-day operations. At a minimum, make sure you have a review and approval system in place so you will not be blindsided when problems or issues arise.

MAKING DIFFICULT DECISIONS

Much of the business of the board is straightforward. But when you face uncertainty or a difficult situation, the two key resources to turn to are your bylaws and your condominium lawyer.

Many questions or issues can be decided by referring to existing policies and laws, including the Condominium Act, Regulations, the Bylaws, and Policies. Some jurisdictions may have additional laws, acts, or regulation and some may have less. Refer to these first as most of the time the answer is right there, black on white.

In your bylaws, you'll find answers to questions such as how often the board is required to meet. Can the board issue fines if the owner doesn't follow the bylaws? What is the owner and what is the board responsible for? Can an owner rent out their unit? Your bylaws are the governing document which will provide you with many answers.

THE BOARD IS ACCOUNTABLE

The board is accountable for its actions. Depending on the jurisdiction, province, or state you reside in, these actions may be subject to legal scrutiny. At times the board's decisions can, and are, challenged by an owner or a group of owners. These challenges can end up in a Court of Law. This is why the board needs to employ or maintain a close relationship with a lawyer that specializes in Condominium Law and seek his or her guidance and advice when needed. Not only to benefit the board but to benefit the corporation as a whole.

A note on management companies: If a condominium management company is managing the corporation the responsibilities of The board may differ because the management company is fulfilling them. Make sure you understand the legal ramifications of this.

For example, instead of the president or secretary communicating with owners on a daily basis the management company may take over this task. Procedures will vary depending on the agreement a board has with a management company. Regardless of your arrangement with your management company, the buck still stops at the board. It is the board who bears the responsibilities, so make sure your arrangement is sound and is serving the best interests of the condominium.

CHAPTER 2

BOARD MEETINGS THAT WORK FOR EVERYONE

S ad to say, there are a few characters you'll find at board meetings that spoil the soup for everyone. Their disrespectful demeanor and self-centered behavior can delay and even prevent the board from accomplishing its important tasks in a timely manner.

From the beginning, make a decision not to be the person who:

- ✔ walks in late and is unprepared to vote on key issues
- ✔ insists on talking out of turn
- ✔ texts (sometimes under the table as if no one noticed!)
- ✔ CANNOT resist offering their opinion on every topic
- ✔ has conversations on the side with another member.

My first condo board meeting was quite interesting. The new business section on the agenda was about a page long and contained items that had been apparently tabled for months. People seemed to put forth their own opinion on every item we needed to discuss yet nobody seemed interested in resolving issues and making decisions. It was clear that the president who was running the meeting had lost control a long time ago.

What was your experience like?

Well, if you were among the majority of new directors when you joined your condominium board, you probably had no prior board experience. You didn't know how a meeting was run, understand its structure, or how to be a productive member. You might even, as I did, found yourself sitting back and wondering: *When will this meeting end?*

If your meetings are longer than an hour then you have some work to do. In this chapter, you'll get an overview of the basics to help you make your meetings as short and efficient as possible.

THE CONDO'S BEST INTEREST

Although the president or designated chairperson is responsible for running the meeting, *everyone on the board must take a position of responsibility* to ensure the meeting stays properly focused. That position is simple:

EVERY BOARD MEMBER IS REQUIRED TO ACT IN THE BEST INTEREST OF THE CONDO.

It's natural to want to join the board to have more say in the running of the condo, but owners who join the board, and do their best to stay on the board, only so they can act in their own self-interest, do a disservice to everyone.

As a board member, if you allow a decision to be made that benefits one individual and not everyone as a whole, and this decision is recorded in the minutes, every other owner will expect the same treatment. You can't say yes to one and no to the other. As an example, if you decide to replace one owner's windows but refuse the others, or let someone keep that extra pet that's not allowed in the bylaws, others will expect the same treatment.

Next time it comes to making a decision and you're unsure, ask yourself this question: "Are we acting in the best interest of everybody as a whole, or are we acting to benefit one or more individuals?"

THE ANATOMY OF A BOARD MEETING

In chapter one, you became familiar with the basic functions of the board, from reviewing owner requests and enforcing by-laws to approving payments and hiring vendors to make repairs. Now we're going to take a look into the nuts and bolts of the meeting itself, which is the structure used for making decisions. *Making decisions is the key function of your monthly board meeting.*

Most board meetings are run in a similar pattern. The meeting is called to order by the president or designated chairperson, who asks if there are any additions or deletions to the agenda. Reports are given by the president, treasurer, secretary, and committee chairs if any, and approved by all. Old business is handled, followed by new business. The meeting is adjourned.

Additionally, it is common for each condominium to have specific laws or protocols that regulate how the board meeting should be run. So make sure you consult your bylaws, regulations, or Condominium Act that may apply.

1—Send an agenda out to all Board Directors at least one week prior to the Monthly Meeting.

An agenda plays a huge role in making sure the meeting is organized and everyone is prepared. This role usually falls to the president but may also be handled by the chairperson or secretary. As long as you have one person responsible for this task and the board is satisfied with the person performing this task, you're on a good path.

Include the minutes from the last meeting and an agenda for the upcoming meeting. Also include any committee reports, financial statements, or background research that the board will need to refer to or discuss at the meeting.

Many times when a board has a meeting it is the first time board directors are presented with quotes, new information, or complaints. This is a big waste of time. Everyone needs to have the opportunity to review this information *before* the meeting. Otherwise, items will most likely be tabled and left on your agenda to discuss at the next meeting.

2—Start (and end) the Board Meeting on time.

Convening promptly will set your meeting on a good trajectory. Members appreciate their time being respected and it sets a positive, productive tone. When meetings start late and go on beyond the time set for closing, the message sent is one of inefficiency and disorganization. Bad habits like these do not support the atmosphere of a well-run meeting. When people become accustomed to the meeting starting and ending on time, it will also improve their promptness.

To conduct a meeting, a minimum number of board directors, called a quorum, are required to be in attendance. Check your bylaws. The quorum requirement will vary, depending on whether it's a Monthly Board Meeting or an Annual General Meeting.

3—Who can attend meetings?

Your condo's bylaws and regulations govern who can attend the Monthly Meeting. In some jurisdictions, the owners may join the meeting and in others, the monthly board meetings are closed to the owners. The advantage of a closed meeting ensures that private or confidential information isn't disclosed to parties that should not have access to certain information, for example, owners' personal contact information or financial state.

However, it is common practice for condo boards to allow owners to directly address the board meeting with issues or requests. Many condo boards set aside fifteen to thirty minutes at the beginning of each board meeting to allow owners to present their concerns.

Make sure the owner is informed of the time they can attend during which you should suspend other business.

Once the presentation is over, the board should ask any additional questions to help them make a proper decision. Then let the owner know that the board will discuss their concern and will get back to them with a decision within a certain time frame.

4—Record the meeting.

The purpose of board meeting minutes is to officially document actions taken by the board of directors. Best practice is for meeting minutes to be brief and capture board business conducted, including motions and votes, but not a summary of the discussion that occurred beforehand.

When recording minutes, the secretary should remember that they are public knowledge and can be requested by anyone. This is why minutes should be brief and to the point, as they could affect the value of units if not recorded properly or if too much information is disclosed to a potential buyer that isn't educated in or familiar with condominiums. Additionally, there may be cases where meeting minutes will be required in a court of law, therefore, you must record all passed motions and any reports that were received.

Once the meeting minutes are reviewed and approved by the board at the beginning of each meeting, it is a good practice to distribute the meeting minutes to all owners. This will increase trust between the board and the owners as well as provide all owners with an update on what is happening within their condo corporation or association.

5—Handle potential Conflicts of Interests up front.

All board directors are required to vote yes or no on every motion unless a conflict of interest exists. If an important matter or decision is about to be discussed, the chairperson should ask if there exists any conflict of interest among the board directors on the topic.

If so, the chairperson will ask the director to temporarily leave the meeting room during the board's discussion and debate. This will ensure that the board of directors can discuss the issue freely and without pressure or guilt. Once a decision has been made the director can rejoin the meeting.

6—Stick to the agenda.

The agenda has a set structure from month to month. It contains items or topics to be discussed and the order in which they will be discussed. Always follow the order of the agenda so the meeting will stay on track. If you would like to add an item to discuss which is not on the agenda, ask the chairperson to add the item under new business at the start of the meeting.

Regardless of good intentions, however, it's very easy for a discussion to go off topic. At this point, the chairperson needs to respectfully interrupt the conversation and move everyone on to the next item.

7—Make a motion!

What makes board meetings different from other meetings is that nothing is ever discussed until a motion is made. When someone would like to propose an action on a topic or item from the agenda, the person will have to make a motion. The motion should be specific, unique, and concise, as well as contain all the relevant details and none of the irrelevant ones.

Another director of the board, or in the case of an Annual General Meeting an owner, must second the motion. This will ensure that the board does not spend time evaluating a proposal that only one person favors. When a motion is seconded, the chairperson will open the floor for debate and discussion. Once the debate is over, the chairperson will ask for a raise of hands of those that are in favor and those that are against. If most votes are in favor the motion is carried and a decision is made. (For more detailed guidelines, refer to Robert's Rules of Orders, which covers all aspects of board meeting protocol.)

When discussing and debating a motion, *always* follow the five guidelines.
- ✔ Listen to the other side
- ✔ Focus on issues, not personalities
- ✔ Be concise
- ✔ Avoid questioning motives
- ✔ Be respectful and polite.

Not every issue will be voted upon. Some require further research and may be tabled to the next meeting.

8—Hold the Annual General Meeting

The Annual General Meeting, distinct from the Monthly Condo Board Meeting, is required by law and is open to all owners. The main purpose of this annual gathering is to inform shareholders and unit owners of the board's business, such as the current state of the condo's finances and any planned projects or ongoing capital improvements being considered. It is also a time to 1) elect new board members, 2) vote on changes in management or staff, and 3) encourage owners and shareholders to ask questions or present issues of concern.

WHAT HAPPENS IN BETWEEN BOARD MEETINGS?

If you really want to keep meetings as short and efficient as possible you'll need to be involved in between board meetings. If there are any new tasks that arise from the meeting, such as requiring quotes for repairs, it's good practice to keep a list of items or tasks that need to be completed by the next meeting.

It's important to have an effective process and system implemented so that when a task is assigned, it can be easily updated and viewed by everyone. For example, if the board wants three quotes for a new lobby carpet, you could assign this task to a condo manager, or a board director. Once the person has updates, such as a new quote, they can inform everyone right away that there's new information for review through the use of a condominium portal. This will aid the board in making quicker and smarter decisions, even between meetings, which in return will shorten your board meetings.

If you take the time to follow these guidelines, you'll consistently enjoy short and efficient meetings.

FREE RESOURCE

1. Agenda and Minutes Template — Download at www.CondoBoardBook.com/toolkit

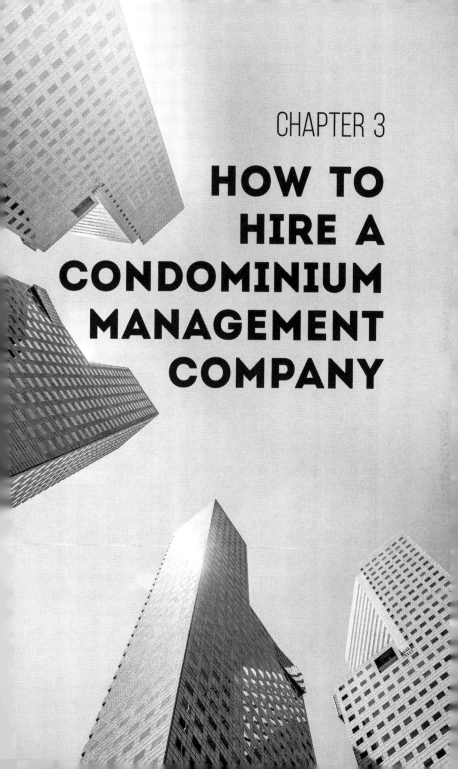

CHAPTER 3

HOW TO HIRE A CONDOMINIUM MANAGEMENT COMPANY

There are bad, good, and great condo management companies out there. The reason I joined our condominium board was because of a bad one. Our condo was mismanaged, tasks did not get done; owners' calls, e-mails, and concerns went unanswered.

Today, I'm happy to report, our board works with an excellent management company that's doing the job we want it to do. And doing it well. This chapter will guide you through a step by step process to help you choose the right management company that fits your condo's needs.

If you're considering hiring a new management company, the first question you may find yourself asking is: Do we even need a condo management company? Boards usually consider the option of self-managing their condominium for two reasons: 1) they are dissatisfied with a previous or current company's management and 2) they want to save money.

Self-management, however, brings risks that a board may not realize right away. Time and Expertise are not on your side. Most board directors don't have the time needed to take care of all the tasks and functions required to manage the condo (refer to the list in chapter 1) , from issuing fines to collecting fees to hiring contractors, and supervising work.

Even greater than time is the problem of expertise. Most board directors have little if any experience sitting on a condo board, let alone the expertise or skills necessary for condominium management. As a starter, when a board chooses to self-manage, directors must possess human relations experience, an accounting background, ability to understand investments, construction standards, skill in managing employees, and knowledge of contracts.

So when boards ask me if they should self-manage their condominium or hire a professional management company, I always recommend they hire a professional company that specializes in condominium management, not just general property management.

PITFALL TO AVOID

Choosing a condo management company is one of the most important jobs that your condo board will undertake. So before laying out the qualifying process that ensures you find a good match, be forewarned of a common pitfall that boards fall prey to.

When boards hire a management company there's a strong tendency to leave everything in the hands of the condo manager. This is a huge mistake. Always remember that the management company is an employee of the condominium corporation. They are required to act on the board's recommendations and not vice versa. The board still needs to be in charge of the decision making, set policies, and make sure bylaws and policies are followed.

DO YOUR HOMEWORK

How will we choose the right company? Is their service really going to be better than with the previous one? Will they take care of our condo as if it were their own?

The answer to these critical questions depends on how well you do your homework, which consists of two main tasks:
- ✔ Understand the needs of your condo, and
- ✔ Select candidates best able to fill those needs.

1—Check your bylaws.

Before beginning the process, review your bylaws for regulations and guidelines. In some jurisdictions, depending on the number of units in a condo corporation, or the size of the budget, the board must hire a professional management company to manage the condo corporation. In other jurisdictions, it's up to the board if they would like to hire a management company or not.

2—Create a list of the board's requirements and prioritize from top to bottom.

Setting clear expectations and requirements that you need from a condo manager is the first critical step to ensuring that you hire the right company. On your list, be sure to include all the services you are expecting from the manager, including qualifications, standards of performance, and levels of service.

Some of the common tasks of a manager are: fee collection, issuing of warnings, fines and letters, managing projects, overseeing maintenance, enforcing rules, responding to emergencies, communicating with owners and tenants, providing a manager's report or updates since the last board meeting, providing financial statements and reports, advising the board of good management practices, alerting the board of any maintenance, collections, rules or other issues that required the board's input and decision.

If there is something specific your board would like to the manager to do, include it. Once you have created your list, prioritize it. Knowing your priorities will help you select the prospective management companies to review.

3—Create a list of prospective management companies.

Start off by reaching out to your network of board directors and colleagues for feedback and recommendations. Select condos that are the same type and size as yours. For example, if your condominium has 30 units, you won't want to consider a company that typically manages 300 units. Once you have a list, ask the boards what their experiences are with that company and if they're happy with the service. Of course, you'll also want to do research on your own to review other companies in your area.

It is reasonable to expect that most managers will be familiar with your jurisdiction's legislation relating to fire regulations, safety, mechanical requirements, employee relations, building maintenance, and managing contractors. They should also be knowledgeable of common property, special resolutions, assessments, meetings, and other condominium related business.

Once you have a list, make a comparison grid of the services and fees of the top three candidates. (A link to a sample Comparison Grid is provided at the end of this chapter.)

4—Send out an RFP to your top 3 candidates.

A useful tool to help your board find the right company at the right price is the Request for Proposal (RFP). A RFP is simply a more formalized document that lists your requirements plus other information a management company needs to have in order to respond to your request: the location of your property, a site map, description of the property, common facilities, parking, owner to tenant ratio, and any major projects you are anticipating in the near future.

As part of the RFP, specify the contact person, include basic financial information (balance sheet and annual budget), a copy of the bylaws, and a deadline for submissions. As part of their response, ask the manager to provide the board with their management contract, a sample of financial reports, insurance, fees, and references.

5—Stipulate financial policies upfront.

As a safeguard against giving the property manager unlimited access to condominium funds, it is recommended that you state your financial policies upfront. For example, in order to ensure that the board stays in control of spending, you might set a policy that the board must approve any expenditure above $1000.00. This practice ensures that the board stays aware of any major expenses.

It also protects the condominium from misuse of funds. I know of instances where management companies have misused or stolen funds from a condo corporation's accounts, hired their preferred vendors and contractors from which they received kickbacks. In some cases, invoices for services were paid before the work was even started.

6—Don't select a company solely based on price.

A mistake that many boards make when selecting a management company is to choose a company based on price. They figure that a management company which charges more will provide a better service, or, conversely, they want to save money and so select a company that charges less.

This isn't always the case. A company that charges less on a monthly contract might have hidden fees for other services.

This happened with a company I once worked with. Our monthly contract fee was quite low, however, we were charged large sums of money for additional work such as maintenance, which was mediocre at best. Since we paid less, we got less time allocated to our condominium, resulting in work not completed on time, concerns going unanswered, and so on.

Our board now works with a company that charges twice what we paid before, but there aren't any hidden fees, and we couldn't be happier. Everything is completed on time, our owners are super happy with the level of service and the board is very satisfied with the professionalism and the quick turnaround from our manager. In the end, we ended up paying about the same for services.

Look carefully at each company's fee structure, especially if your budget is tight, as you want to avoid paying less upfront, but getting hit later with additional fees that may accumulate without your knowledge. Verify if the company charges extra for services such as meetings, documents, maintenance, travel time, etc.

7—Interview companies.

Your next step is to interview each management company on your list. The good management companies will be interviewing your board as well. This is where you'll realize if the company actually wants to work with you and help you, or just wants your money. A good company will ensure that they can provide the right service for your board and your condo corporation before handing you a contract to sign.

When interviewing, always ask for the manager that will manage your condominium to be present at the meeting. During the initial interview a company usually sends the owner of the company or a senior manager, and once the contract is signed a different person may show up to manage your property.

8—Create a set of questions.

Create a set of questions to ask every company. Make sure to include a couple of questions that deal with common problems that most condominiums face.   It's a good barometer for measuring how different companies handle similar situations. For example, "How would you deal with an owner who's not paying his or her condo or association fees?"

Honesty is important for both sides in order to build trust between your board and the management company from the beginning. So make sure you are clear about your requirements and that you get all your questions answered to your satisfaction. If you have a request that is out of the ordinary, negotiate it upfront and work to come to a mutual agreement.

9—Get a legal review of the contract.

Once the board decides on a management company and a manager, have the contract or agreement reviewed by your condo corporation's lawyer. This will be an additional expense but one worth investing in. Your lawyer will advise you if there are any red flags and ensure that the contract is structured to benefit both parties.

When everything is ready to go, signed, and you are working with a new manager, make sure you have a tool or process whereby the manager can log any tasks, requests from owners, maintenance issues, etc. This will provide the board with a clear picture of what's happening within the condo corporation, help you be more pro-active, as well as track the performance of the manager. Make sure the tool tracks when a project was created, completed, and any updates associated with each task.

If you go through these steps with diligence and thoroughness, you will have done your condo a great service!

FREE RESOURCE

1. Comparison Grid – Download at
   www.CondoBoardBook.com/toolkit

CHAPTER 4

KEEP YOUR OWNERS INFORMED

One of the most common complaints from owners and residents in the condominium and residential industry is that they have no idea of what's going on in their condo. Fifty-one percent of all owners living in condos complain that they are ill-informed, especially when issues or problems arise. Many will tell you that communication from the board is not only lacking but non-existent.

It was for this reason that I joined my board. I was tired of being kept in the dark and I was afraid of not knowing what might happen to the value of our home in the coming months and years.

As soon I joined the board I quickly realized that communication from the board to its owners was the main problem. It wasn't special assessments. It wasn't repairs. It wasn't water leaks. It wasn't elevator outages. It wasn't a rise in condominium fees. *It was the lack of communication.*

So why is this such a big problem?

The board carries a lot of responsibilities on its shoulders; the list of issues and their complexity can be overwhelming, especially for most board directors who are short on time and expertise. But the board should *never* lose sight that one of its key functions is *to keep owners informed.* Owners will appreciate it and your board (and the condo) will function with harmony and efficiency. The alternative is chaos and never-ending complaints.

So where do you begin to understand and solve this challenging problem?

Let's start by taking a quick look at the underlying causes.

1—TIME.

Board directors lack the time or commitment to make communication a priority. They are volunteers who want to spend as little time as possible working on additional "condo stuff." They believe that attending meetings is enough to ask of them. Beyond that, they become resentful and resistant.

2—INNOVATION.

Boards aren't typically innovative enough to figure out how to solve their communication problems—and they are afraid of change. As a result, problems become worse, complaints increase, often making board members lives miserable.

I was one of those owners myself when I got up and released my fury at the first Annual General Meeting I ever attended. In the face of the barrage of continual and angry complaints, I understand why board members can get discouraged, and why their willingness to help and participate decreases over time.

3—FEAR OF ACCOUNTABILITY.

A board's lack of communication is often intentional. Board directors can become afraid of what the owners will think of their decisions and how they're running the condominium. Similarly, management companies can fall into this trap by neglecting to inform the board about the progress of tasks or issues, in the (usually false) hope that the board won't hold them accountable for their actions or lack thereof.

4–LACK OF FEEDBACK.

Without proper feedback from the owners, the board doesn't always know if they're making the right decision. We as board members try to make the best decision with the information we have been presented. However, at times the information simply isn't enough.

Here's an example of how good communication can make all the difference.

Several years ago our condo board decided to give our gym a little facelift. We were thinking of replacing older equipment with some new gear. At the board meeting, we looked at everything that was in the gym but were uncertain what to replace. Some gear was still in good shape, some looked like it was in good shape, but none of the board members used the gym on a regular basis. Our budget didn't allow us to replace everything, so we decided to ask our owners for suggestions. We received quite a bit of constructive feedback and our decision ended up being quick and painless, to everyone's satisfaction.

Communication is more than just informing owners of what is happening. It's part of running a successful condominium. Since most board members don't have the experience running a condo, communicating with the owners is one of the most valuable channels for getting feedback and advice to help the board make the proper decisions.

Open channels from the board to the owners also create transparency. Transparency, in turn, generates trust. This doesn't mean you ask owners or your community for feedback on every decision you make, but it means that you keep them in the loop. The result is they will feel you care about them and are genuinely looking out for their interests, and that the right people are at the helm. You'll find, as trust builds, that complaints will naturally decrease.

Keep in mind that most people complain and get angry about a problem or situation because they don't understand it. If they don't understand what's going on, people inevitably start coming to their own conclusions. Gossip spreads and people make up stories that have little basis in reality. We see the same thing on TV shows, social media sites, and various news channels, where conclusions are constantly being reached without the benefit of all the information.

WHAT SHOULD YOU COMMUNICATE TO OWNERS AND RESIDENTS?

Now that you have an understanding of the underlying problem, let's talk about possible solutions. First, we'll take a look at the "what" followed by the "how." The *what* focuses on what information you need to communicate to owners, while the *how* addresses the means and best practices for doing so.

1. NOTICES.

Notices or alerts that are provided to owners or residents need to be informative. If a notice only states that "Water will be shut off on Monday," it will create more questions and concerns—and residents will naturally start to worry. If you provide more detail, such as: "Water will be shut off on Monday, Wednesday, and Friday due to the replacement of piping to prevent future water damage and leaks to units and common property," your community will understand why such maintenance is required. Thus, fewer questions and complaints will result. It's a win-win for everyone.

2. CHANGES IN THE BOARD OF DIRECTORS.

When a director joins or leaves the board or a position changes, such as a new president is elected, let your owners know right away. This makes owners feel comfortable in knowing that there is someone looking after their home, their investment, and capably taking care of the day-to-day operations of the condominium.

3. CHANGES IN POLICIES OR BYLAWS.

Don't delay in informing owners of important changes in policies or bylaws. If owners aren't aware of new rules, you can hardly expect them to comply. You don't want people to be surprised when they receive a letter from the board or the property manager informing them of an infraction or a fine they knew nothing about.

4. MAINTENANCE.

You need to keep your residents and community informed at all times of any maintenance issues or work that affects their unit or common property, such as the elevators, the garage doors, security systems, access to the building, and so on. Make sure everybody knows about these in advance. You don't want to be the kind of board that informs the owners the day of the repair or shutdown. Give owners several days notice and keep them updated as work progresses. Otherwise, you will constantly receive complaints from angry owners.

Of course, there are emergencies that can't be planned for or anticipated but let owners know as soon as possible with an explanation of what has happened. As long as they are informed and provided with updates it's more likely they will trust the process and your decisions.

5. CHANGES IN FINANCES OR MAJOR EXPENSES.

One of the most important areas to communicate to your owners is any change in finances or major expenses. Especially when you are planning to increase contribution fees, such as condo fees. Most owners don't understand how condo fees work and what they are used for. So it's critical that the board not only give owners a heads up but also provides a clear explanation as to why such an increase is necessary.

Utilities, insurance fees, and labor prices go up. It's the nature of business. However if your owners only receive a notice that the monthly fees are going up, without an explanation, they're going to get angry. They may blame the board of directors, and it's likely they will start questioning every single decision the board makes. They'll start asking, "Why are our fees constantly going up? Is the board collecting the money and putting it into their own pockets? Are they paying themselves? What's going on?"

6. THE ANNUAL GENERAL MEETING.

In order to ensure a good turnout, give owners a 30-day notice of the Annual General Meeting (AGM) and other events. Their participation is valuable, as it aids the board in understanding issues and making good decisions. It also creates goodwill and trust, which makes the board's job easier.

Some boards that I've worked with are very strict on the rules and say, "Our bylaws state that we only have to give 15 days' notice and that's all we're going to give." Condominiums are not a monarchy. Remember, you live in the same community as your neighbors do, so be considerate and understanding. Give owners a little bit of notice so they can actually plan for this event. It will also help ensure that you meet the quorum required. Otherwise, you may have to reschedule the meeting.

7. COMMITTEE MEETINGS.

Make sure you also inform your owners and residents about committee meetings. Whether it's communications committee, a membership committee, or an events committee, let your owners know so they have a chance to attend and perhaps volunteer and contribute their energy and expertise to helping the condo run better. You never know when you'll get that one great owner that will change things for the better.

Additionally, make an effort to inform your owners and residents about neighborhood events and activities. This is a good task for the communications committee. When owners participate in such events, it builds a strong community and helps owners feel a part of something bigger.

HOW TO OPEN THE COMMUNICATIONS CHANNEL

Knowing what to communicate is fairly straightforward. Knowing how to do it, however, is a bit more complicated, at least in the beginning. Let's start with some basic principles.

MAKE IT EASY.

Communication with your community needs to be quick and simple. You don't want this process to take up too much of the board's or manager's time. It should be as easy as sending an email. If it takes hours to produce and distribute a notice within a property, no one will want to step up to do it.

BE TIMELY.

Think of your communications as news releases. The sooner you let everyone know what's happening the more impact these news announcements will have. Imagine if you heard ground breaking news days, weeks, or months after an event had occurred. It wouldn't hold much meaning, would it? If news channels or newspapers took this approach they wouldn't be in business very long.

However, this is exactly the approach many condominium boards take. They feel that releasing a quarterly newsletter is enough. However, by the time the owners and residents receive a newsletter the information is outdated and no longer relevant.

TONE.

When communicating with your owners make sure that you are using the right tone in your message. Be friendly and understanding. After all, you too are an owner. If you weren't a board director think of how you would like your board to communicate with you in a perfect world.

CREATE TEMPLATES.

Your board sends out the same type of notices or communications over and over: maintenance alerts, meetings announcements, changes in policies, to name a few. To save time and ensure timeliness, create a process and a template that anyone can follow for each type of communication.

Specify the type of information you'll include in your communiqué, what time of the day it will go out, the day it will go out. Decide if it will be a letter, an email, or a post on your private communication portal. The more details you include in your steps the easier it will be for a board member to follow and execute, especially if they are new. Creating these templates is a good task for the secretary or the communications committee to take on.

PAPER VS. DIGITAL: WHICH IS BEST?

When communicating with the owners most boards still resort to paper notices. They can be effective, however, there are a couple of things you need to consider. To post a paper notice, you have to be on the property or travel to it, then tape it to elevators, doors, mailboxes, and so on. These notices are often so long that residents don't even have the time to fully read them, especially when they're coming home, tired, after a full day of work. People often write awful messages on the notice and eventually it gets torn down by an angry owner. You could slide notices under every door, but this will cost you not only time but money, but a sore back.

You may be thinking, "Well that's great, so how do I communicate with everyone? And what about the owners living offsite?" The simplest way, but most time consuming and expensive, is to mail a letter. Depending on the type of information you are sending out, it's important to check the bylaws in your jurisdiction to see if a physical letter is required by law. There are additional costs associated with physical mail, therefore, a secondary option to communicating with owners offsite could be an online communication portal. This option is being adopted by more condominiums every single month.

THE IMMEDIACY OF TECHNOLOGY

In this day and age, people want and expect information *now*. When it's current, when it's fresh. Sometimes they want it yesterday so they can be the first to know the latest and greatest. Smart phones, tablets, and computers are tools that most people use to consume the latest news and information. What's more, the use of technology is no longer limited to a certain age group. The number of retirees becoming familiar with these tools and technology is growing each month.

Communicating with residents and owners using technology like smart phones that the most people are familiar with and use every day is to the board's advantage because you'll not only save time and money, you will build goodwill and trust.

Just imagine. What if informing your owners and residents was quick and painless? No need to print and post a notice all over your property. Instead, residents would receive a notice within seconds and would have an archive of notices they could refer to at a later time. (If you post a notice on the common property and it gets torn down, then it's gone. At times owners will not even see it.)

However many Boards are often afraid of technology. They think of social media and start to panic. I understand why.

Social media tools such as Facebook, Twitter, and Instagram aren't the best option for condominiums. I highly advise against using these tools because they are designed for public consumption. For example, if you have a Facebook site available for anyone to post on, you have no control over who starts a conversation. An owner might post something about water flooding or complain about the rise of condo fees. These postings have multiple damaging effects. They can lower the value of the condo property and even affect someone's decision to purchase a unit if the information gets out. Posts like this also undermine owners' confidence in the board's ability to do their job.

The best option for condominiums is a private communication portal. This is a place where your owners feel part of your community. A place where all communication is happening behind a closed door. Behind a secure login.

If you're thinking, "This won't work for us. We don't have the time to set something up like this, and beside our owners are older, don't have computers and prefer paper notices." Well, take a deep breath, because you're in for a major eye opening.

I've helped hundreds of condos with communication problems since 2010 across Canada and The United States, working with residents from the age of 18 to 85. You'd be surprised how many residents prefer to receive their information electronically. Why? Well, they can receive notices at work. They can receive notices at school. They can receive notices if they live offsite. And they can receive notices without leaving their home. They can also get notices when they're on vacation.

As soon as we provided our owners with an online portal with the goal of improving our communications the number of complaints, questions and inquiries dropped drastically. So did the time we had been spending to keep up with the information we were required to communicate.

SIMPLICITY, SIMPLICITY, SIMPLICITY

When looking for a tool to help you set up a communication system that works for owners, the board, and the condominium manager, it can't be overemphasized that it needs to be *very* simple to use. The tool has to be as easy as writing an email. It has to be simple enough so that when a new board director joins, or a new manager takes over your property, they will be able to jump in and immediately run with it.

Other important requirements include:

- ✔ The ability to make all communications as transparent as possible while protecting individual privacy.
- ✔ Unlimited technical support and a toll-free phone number that everyone has access to. If your owners have questions, or if they cannot log in or access information, be certain that there's someone on the other end of the email or phone call that will handle support for you. You don't want owners e-mailing or calling board members for technical help.

Some directors advocate building their own website. I strongly advise against this because when a board director develops a custom website, they're usually the only one who knows how to run and maintain it. So when the director leaves there's no one to take over. Besides, you don't want the board to take on this type of responsibility.

USE TEXT MESSAGING AND AUTOMATED PHONE CALLS

Text messaging, also known as SMS, and automated phone calls are two additional tools to have access to, especially useful for reminders and updates, such as upcoming meetings or emergency maintenance. You type a message, click a button, and the SMS or text message is instantly sent to all your owners. The process is similar for automated calls.

Not everyone has a computer, but the majority of people these days, including seniors, have a smart phone or cell phone. If one of your owners doesn't have either, you can arrange to send messages to their family members; and the family members can then inform the owner of any updates.

A couple of years ago I was on vacation, and while relaxing on a beach on the other side of the world I received a notice from my condominium board that there was flooding in the lower level parking, where our car was parked. As soon as I received this notice I called my friend who was looking after our condo. He checked our car and discovered that our parking stall wasn't affected. But to avoid any problems he moved our vehicle to above ground parking. Without an electronic system, this kind of proactive support would not have been possible.

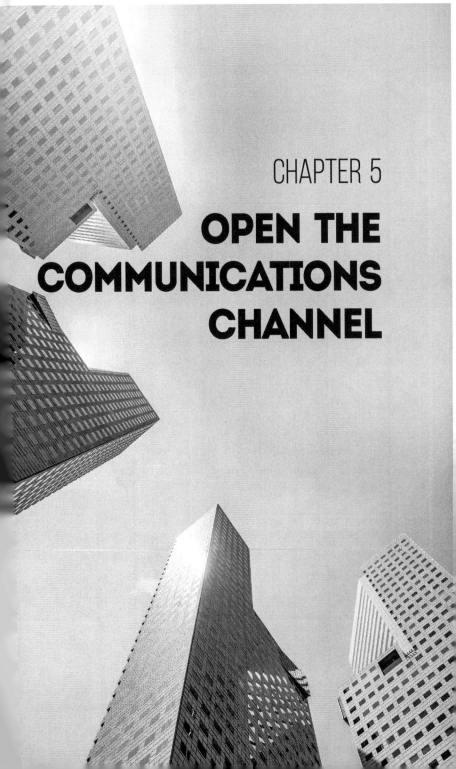

CHAPTER 5

OPEN THE COMMUNICATIONS CHANNEL

Adopting a system that keeps owners and residents informed of events and important information is a significant accomplishment for any board. But there's more to communication than that: the channel needs to go both ways.

Have you ever found yourself in a situation where you contacted your board of directors, or your manager, then didn't hear back from them? How did that make you feel? When I moved into my newly purchased condo back in 2003, I had a lot of questions. Who do I contact during emergencies? What are the rules and regulations? Where are the bylaws? Eventually, I did receive a reply. Four months later! By that time, I was understandably furious.

Are you surprised? If you aren't, then you know exactly what I'm talking about and this is what we'll be discussing in this chapter.

The third largest problem in residential associations is unanswered questions or concerns by owners and residents. In fact, an astonishing *thirty-five percent of all owners* don't hear back from the board or manager. That's over a third of owners living in condominiums in North America!

Most boards and managers defend themselves by saying, "We read all emails and listen to every single voicemail we receive." But that's not much reassurance if owners never receive a specific reply to their inquiry.

How responsive is your board or manager? Do owners receive a prompt reply? Are they informed that the issue is being looked into or are their concerns left unanswered?

Owners want and deserve to know what is happening with their issues and concerns. If they don't receive a reply or acknowledgment, they will assume that no one got the message or worse, that they're being ignored. As a result, they will keep calling and emailing in an attempt to get an answer or an update. This is extremely time consuming, frustrating and stressful, for both the owner and the board or manager.

WHAT'S HAPPENING HERE?

Let's look at a typical process that most condo boards have in place for dealing with inquiries or complaints.

1. A call or an email is received and it is added to the bottom of the TO DO list. (I hope it's a list and not a bunch of sticky notes on the wall which I've actually seen!)
2. If the issue requires a discussion at the board level it is queued up until the next board meeting. (Meanwhile, owners are waiting, and continuing to call and email for an update.)
3. The board makes a decision and a reply is sent to the owner, that is if someone decides to reply to the owner, which doesn't always happen.

With this kind of dysfunctional system, it's easy to see how *the time between request and reply can turn into weeks and even months.*

EMPOWER YOUR BOARD TO HANDLE ALL OWNER COMMUNICATIONS

The first step to eliminating this bottleneck is to make sure the board handles responses to owners, instead of the condo manager. If the board isn't aware of incoming messages from owners, it's difficult to know if your property manager is actually doing their job. Certain issues may never be brought to the board's attention, especially if they put the manager in a bad light.

Board directors may balk at assuming this task because they're afraid it's going to require time and expertise they don't have. However, in the end, you will actually save time—and it can be simple to implement.

When I joined our board, our meetings were between two and three hours long. As soon as we implemented a solution to track and respond to the concerns and problems that our owners were having, we were able to address them easily between our meetings, which resulted in meetings that were one hour or shorter.

Another key advantage to having the board responds to owners instead of the manager is information access.

Condo management companies change and when they do, the board loses access to the history of owners' complaints, concerns, and requests. This history is valuable, especially for new board members who join the board with no prior understanding of how a board operates and what kinds of problems it deals with every day.

Here are simple guidelines for an effective response to an owner request or complaint. Following these guidelines achieves multiple objectives. First, it solves problems before they become serious and unmanageable. Second, you build trust and confidence in the ability of the board to govern well. And third, your job as a board director becomes fulfilling and can even be enjoyable.

- ✔ Respond immediately to an owner's message. Decide what your policy will be (same-day or 24 hours, for example) and communicate it to owners, so there are no surprises.

- ✔ Acknowledge that you have received their message, even if you don't have an immediate answer to their concern. This simple confirmation shows the owner or the resident that you have heard them and actually care about what they have to say.

- ✔ Keep owners updated on the progress of the issue. This will prevent or at least reduce the barrage of inquiries requesting a status. If the property manager is taking care of an issue within a tracked system, it will be easy for them to inform everyone of actions being taken.

- ✔ Track the date the message was received, the date of response, who took action, and how the issue was resolved. This history will provide you with valuable insight into what's really going on in your condominium and how to solve similar issues in the future.

GET SUPPORT FROM THE CONDO MANAGER

Initially, your condo manager may oppose the board taking on the responsibility of tracking messages. This is the time to remember that the manager is the employee of the condo corporation whose job it is to follow the board's guidance and recommendations, not vice versa.

The usual reason for the manager's resistance is because it creates transparency. I have found that managers open up to this idea when they realize it will make their job easier. Help your manager understand that an open channel of communication will help them track and handle concerns, as well as reducing complaints in the long run.

WHAT'S THE BEST SYSTEM TO USE?

Email is the most common solution that boards and managers use today to track owners' messages and replies. Folders get created and emails moved around. If there aren't too many messages or only one or two people are managing the emails, this system is fairly workable. However, within a typical condo environment, this is not the case. There may be eight board directors who are communicating back and forth, searching through multiple email threads and trying to figure out what the status is. This process can quickly become a nightmare for everyone.

Which brings us back to the solution we discussed in the previous chapter which I recommend over email: *A private communication portal*. The guidelines for handling inbound communications are the same: Make it easy. Be timely. Use a friendly tone. Create templates that include the details that should be included in your message.

Whatever solution you decide to use, make sure you have a simple thread for messages, replies, and comments. It should be similar to an online chat that is stored and displayed in historical order so it's very clear what the latest status is. For example, if a board director replies at 1:00 pm and another director replies at 1:05 pm, the 1:05 pm reply will be underneath the 1:00 pm reply.

Several years ago one of our owners submitted a message that he heard water dripping inside of the wall. We started investigating but couldn't find anything. Then another message came in from another owner, and another, and another. By communicating with the owners that informed us of the issue we were able to locate a pinhole leak in one of the pipes within the wall. Being proactive allowed us to address and solve this problem before we had a major flood through six floors. We saved thousands of dollars in repair costs.

SOME PROBLEMS DON'T GO AWAY

A good communication system is an enormous boost for efficiency and satisfaction for all around, but it's important to realize that there are challenges that don't go away. Even when owners receive a prompt reply and update, when there's a problem, they will be concerned, they may be aggravated, they will likely be angry.

The biggest reason is that most owners and residents are uneducated and uninformed about how condominiums function. They don't really know what it takes to run a condo corporation. They think things can be simply fixed by a snap of a finger, so when you're replying to these messages make it a priority to be friendly and courteous in your language, and provide as much information as possible about an issue.

CHAPTER 6

PROVIDE EASY ACCESS TO IMPORTANT DOCUMENTS

mportant information that owners want and need is usually spread across various documents such as meeting minutes, bylaws and policies. Generally, easy access is not provided, and it's not unusual for owners to be charged a fee to obtain copies.

Before I joined the board of our condominium, I had no access to documents. I didn't even know where this information was kept. For example, when I had a question about the policy for visitor parking I had no idea where to go. Other questions, like "How do I book the amenity room?" or "Where can I get a copy of the bylaws?" were the same. I was clueless.

Thirty-three percent of all owners complain regularly that they don't have access to this kind of important information. It is the second largest complaint in residential associations. If your board doesn't provide access to this information, you have a problem, a big problem.

Many condominium boards and management companies prevent owners from accessing documents or make it very difficult. Owners have a legal right to view and access certain corporation documents, including board meeting minutes, bylaws, and policies.

REASONS FOR ACCESS

If your board and management have a policy of withholding documents or making it difficult for owners to access them, consider the following reasons to change that policy today.

✔ Create transparency.

When you inform your owners through documents, such as meeting minutes, of the decisions the board is making, the owners and the community will start trusting the decisions of the board, because information is not being kept from them.

✔ Ensure accountability.

Another reason is accountability. Many owners believe that the board is a secret society that makes decisions for their own self-interest without considering the interest of the owners. By providing access to such documents, owners will realize that the actions taken by the board for the benefit of the owners.

✔ Reduce complaints.

When owners have access to documents, there will be a reduction in complaints and accusations. Owners will see for themselves the board is doing its job to maintain the condominium, common property, ensuring the value of their investment.

✔ Increase compliance to rules and policies.

Can you really blame owners for not following bylaws, regulations, or policies if they are not given easy access to this information? Or worse, if they are required to pay fees for it?

Once your owners have easy access to rules and regulations, it will be much easier to enforce them. For example, if a rule is being broken, you can refer to it specifically in your news announcement or bulletin, indicating the paragraph in the bylaws or policy document. Since this information is available to everyone, owners can verify it for themselves.

Condo managers will sometimes resist changing this policy, saying they are the owners of the documents. This is a total lie. Remember that the management company is an employee of the corporation. They may be the *holders* of your corporation's documents and records, however, they are not the owners. Documents and records are the property of the condominium corporation.

There are reasons why a management company may make such a claim. First, they want to maintain control of owner access. Second, it allows them to require a "service charge" for providing documents to those that request them, which ends up in their bank account.

When you purchased your condominium, do you remember paying any service, printing, or delivery fees for your documents to close the sale? Of course not. Yet I know of management companies that charge fifty dollars for a set of meeting minutes and up to eight hundred dollars for a full set of documents.

WHAT DOCUMENTS SHOULD BE SHARED?

Not all documents can be shared automatically, as the information required must sometimes be compiled and verified first. In such cases, an owner may have to contact the board or manager.

The majority of documents, however, can be easily shared with owners, and certain documents should also be shared with residents, renters, and tenants. By share, I don't mean, make it available if someone asks for it. These documents should be available "on demand," which means they are available to download 24/7 from a protected website or online portal.

✔ **Board Meeting Minutes.**
The minutes of a board meeting contain critical information that may affect condominium fees, such as, changes to the association or the corporation, upcoming special assessments, major repairs to common property or mechanical equipment. To ensure minutes are being properly and accurately recorded, always have the board secretary record the minutes, not the property manager.

✔ **Policies and Bylaws.**
Owners and residents need to be aware of the rules and regulations of the community they live in. For example, if an owner is fined for a parking violation, they can't rely on the excuse that they didn't know what the rules were.

✔ **Insurance Certificates.**
Insurance certificates can be shared as well and any documents the owner requires for their personal use.

For example, if an owner wants to purchase insurance for their property, make it easy for them to access the information they need.

SHARING AND STORING DOCUMENTS

The board should retain a copy and an original of every single condominium document, including as-built drawings, board meeting minutes, bylaws, policies, vendor contracts, and owner contracts or agreements. Often it's the management company or the property manager that maintains and holds these documents. Occasionally even the board doesn't have access to them.

I know of situations where a board decided to change their management company and the ex-management company didn't want to turn over certain documents to the board. So be forewarned. From the beginning, make sure the board has all the documents.

A very common tool that boards use to store documents are binders. Owners sign out the documents or read them at the office. This method exists because boards usually don't have anyone with the technical skill to make documents available electronically.

When storing copies of your documents make sure all documents are secure. Management companies or boards usually store them in filing cabinets or the secretary stores them at home. You might run into problems with this. I once worked with a condo corporation where the secretary called me in tears and said that during a recent move she had lost two boxes of meeting minutes.

That's why electronic copies are recommended. *Make sure you digitize every single document that you have for the corporation, including board minutes.* If your secretary is taking minutes by hand, have them typed or scanned afterward so they can be saved in a digital format.

The best and most affordable option for storing digital documents is a third party service that only permits people with a secure login to access and view. When sharing documents online make sure the right people have access to the right documents. When you upload a document, whatever online system you use, you should be able to specify who has access to it. Is it the board, is it the owner, or is it the resident?

For example, boards typically make bylaws accessible to everyone while vendors contracts are only viewable by the board or manager. As for meeting minutes, make sure they're accessible to owners but not residents or tenants.

In any case, never post condominium documents on a public or social media website. Documents should be available to your condo community only. When sharing documents, also ensure that personal owner information is retracted from the documents. Owners' information, such as name, address, and financial information should never be visible to the rest of the community. Jurisdictions have different regulations regarding personal information, so obtain legal counsel to ensure you are in compliance.

"I can't open this document!" These are words you never want to hear.

Just because you can open a document does not necessarily mean that everyone will be able to do the same. There are many platforms in use, such as Google, Windows, and Macintosh, along with various smart phone and tablet operating systems. So when sharing documents digitally make sure they're viewable by everyone.

That's why I strongly recommend *saving or exporting every document as a PDF file*. (PDF stands for Portable Document Format.) It is a standard document file on the Internet which anyone can view. In fact, most computers and devices come pre-installed with a PDF viewer, and if they are not, it can be easily downloaded for free on any device. PDF documents are also secure. Although they can be viewed, the contents can't be changed or edited, which makes it an ideal format.

COMMON SCENARIOS FOR HANDLING DOCUMENT REQUESTS

Your board, like your condo manager, is often reluctant to change. They may be able to see the benefits of digital documents, but—as with most organizations—there's a strong tendency to stick with the way they're used to handling things. To give you a true picture of how most boards or managers actually manage these requests, let's run through some typical scenarios for sending the board minutes to owners.

Scenario 1. Request by Phone or E-mail — *Paper Document*

The board has approved the minutes and you have a paper copy. An owner requests the latest minutes over the phone or via e-mail. You verify that the person requesting the minutes is an owner. You search for the document in a file or cabinet and photocopy the document. You put it in an envelope, apply postage, and mail the document. *This task could take fifteen to twenty minutes per request.*

Scenario 2. Request by Phone or E-mail — *Digital Document*

The board has approved the minutes and you have a digital copy. An owner requests the latest minutes over the phone or via e-mail. You verify that the person requesting the minutes is an owner. You open up your e-mail application, select the meeting minutes file from your computer, and e-mail it to the owner who requested the minutes. *This could take five to ten minutes per request.*

Scenario 3: E-mail — *Digital Document*

The board has approved the minutes and you have a digital copy. You open up your e-mail application, select the meeting minutes file from your computer, and e-mail it to all owners simultaneously. *This could take between five to ten minutes in total.*

- ✔ If you use email, make sure that you keep your e-mail list frequently updated so you don't spam people that no longer live in your community.
- ✔ Maintain three separate lists. One for owners, one for tenants/renters, and one for board directors, to ensure that you are sending documents to the proper recipients.

Scenario 4: Private Condominium Communication Portal

The board has approved the minutes and you have a digital copy. You log in to your portal, select the file from your computer, specify who should have access to the minutes and upload the document to the portal. *This will take you about one minute.*

- ✔ The condo portal will automatically inform all owners that a new set of meeting minutes has been uploaded.
- ✔ You don't have to deal with e-mail or phone requests for documents.

So tell me . . . which option sounds best to you?

If your condominium currently has a website, make sure all the owners and residents are informed when new information or new documents are added to the website. You can send out an email, or, if you use the right portal, it will automatically inform the proper people as soon as the document is posted.

USE THE RIGHT TOOL FOR THE RIGHT JOB

Are you ready to look at tools and options that will allow you and your condo manager to share documents with your owners—quickly and easily? Just follow these simple guidelines we've discussed in this chapter.

Select an online portal that is designed for condominiums, specifically for use by board members and managers. Make sure that: 1) documents can be easily uploaded in a secure format (PDF), 2) that you're able to set proper access permissions, and that 3) owners and residents have access to these documents 24/7 without having to contact you.

By sharing the corporate documents, you'll dramatically reduce the number of inquiries *and* the time it takes to respond to those requests. The result will be less volunteer time for the board, more efficiency, and happier owners!

CHAPTER 7

MANAGING AND TRACKING WORK

Before joining our condominium board, I blamed the board and the management company for not doing their job. Other owners felt the same. Was I wrong? I didn't think so. Our property was starting to look run down. Dents and scratches were everywhere, the elevator was unreliable, sometimes the garage door wouldn't open. To make matters worse, the board was not replying to repeated owners' requests and complaints.

Then came time for my first condo board meeting. Eager to get to work, I asked for the current list of work requests or projects, but there wasn't any. The board relied on the condo manager to handle everything. The big shock came when I found out that the manager didn't have a list either.

How could we as a board, as a condominium corporation, hold the property manager accountable?

If the board defaults to letting the condo manager run the show with zero accountability, it's like getting a pet and letting it run loose without feeding it or taking care of it. Eventually, a disaster will happen. In fact, I've discovered that a good portion of newly elected directors do just that. They think that simply by sitting on the board and attending meetings, things will magically get done.

When I ran my own consulting business, every project was tracked and each task assigned to a person with a deadline. If it wasn't completed on time, I was notified automatically, allowing me to find out what the problem was and to see if additional resources were needed.

It's the board's responsibility to ensure that all common property is maintained, and when needed, repaired or replaced. However, the majority of boards don't know when was the last time something was repaired, how often it was repaired, or how much money was spent on repairs. Because there's no tracking record. As a result, repairs continue to be requested and the board may unknowingly waste money on equipment that should have been replaced months or even years ago.

Tracking work requests and tasks is essential to running an effective and successful condo corporation.

CREATE AN EFFICIENT TRACKING PROCESS.

A tracking record empowers the board to make good decisions. Here are the basic elements of every project or task, including work requests, that should be tracked.

✔ **DATE.**
    Recording the date the task was created lets you see how long it takes for a task to be completed, which will help you plan in the future.

✔ **TIME.**
    Anticipate how much time needs to be spent on a task. For example, if the monthly landscaping is expected

to take three hours, but a contractor is billing you for ten, you can question the situation.

✔ COMMENTS and UPDATES.

Track comments and updates associated with each task. If there are any changes that have been discussed or decisions that have been made, include that information as well.

✔ CONTRACTS and DOCUMENTS.

Documents, price quotes, proposals or contracts associated with tasks should be tracked and accessible for review at any time. Having this kind of history will also guide your annual budgeting process.

As a board, you will benefit tremendously by tracking tasks and work requests in your condo corporation. Imagine being able to see what's being done and what problems arise along the way. Tasks and projects may take a little bit longer to complete, but as a board, you'll have the ability to be proactive instead of reactive, and act on issues before they become unmanageable.

You'll learn how your vendors or property managers perform. Instead of adding more items to your to-do list, you'll start to whittle it down. Over time, with an accurate history, you'll be able to manage expectations with more efficiency (and your meetings will be shorter).

Another advantage to tracking work requests is that you become aware of how an issue or problem may affect more than one owner. When you receive multiple complaints or requests about the same issue, you can investigate before it becomes a large-scale problem.

Sometimes condo managers resist the idea of a tracking process. If you have a condo manager who doesn't want to be this transparent, let them know that tracking tasks and work requests will make their job and your job easier. Most property managers manage several properties and have a lot of items to take care of. With an easy-to-use tracking tool, they can keep the board updated on issues, repairs, or requests and they'll have fewer calls or emails to deal with.

A win-win for everyone.

Here's the bottom line. The board's decision to track projects and tasks is essential to running the condominium *as a business*. The Board is the Boss. The condo manager, on the other hand, is an employee of that business. This is a fact many boards get confused about.

Remember, depending on the number of units in your condominium, you may be running a multi-million dollar corporation and you need as much help as possible.

COMMON TRACKING SYSTEMS

There are several ways to track tasks and work requests.

1—Use a spreadsheet.

The simplest way is to create a spreadsheet that includes key information, such as the date requested, the unit associated with it, or the type of mechanical equipment needing repair or replacement. Spreadsheets, however, have a tendency to get very large and unmanageable, especially when more than a few people are updating and adding new information.

2—Adopt a project management tool.

Project management tools are also a good option, but they are more technical. Microsoft Project, for example, is a very robust software application that can handle a lot of information, but learning to use it effectively requires a lot of training. Other downsides? It's not designed specifically for condominiums and the costs are excessive.

3—Use a web-based condominium portal.

A web-based portal geared for the condominiums industry is an ideal option. Since most board directors are not technically savvy, you need a solution that is easy to set up and quick to implement. A tool that's really easy to understand and learn. Something that offers video or online on-demand training, with support so you can talk to someone over the phone when you need help.

MAKE IT EASY FOR THE BOARD TO DO THEIR JOB.

Board directors are volunteers—and they are also busy people who want to help. Make it easy for them, not hard.

Tracking tasks and work requests, especially in a condominium where you're dealing with tens or hundreds of units, is one of the most valuable actions you can take to support your board's effectiveness. Issues and items that need attention will no longer slip through "the cracks." Complaints and owner requests will decrease. Meetings will accomplish what needs to be done in half the time. And board members will feel they are making a contribution—and likely want to do more.

When board members have the kind of information that a tracking tool provides, they have an accurate picture of what's going on in the condo, often for the first time. They are able to make good decisions, decisions that empower the board to run a successful condominium.

CHAPTER 8

THE
NEXT STEP

Here are some thoughts condo board directors have had while reading this book.

While reading this book have you had the following thoughts?

"I wish we could run better condo board meetings!"

"I wish we didn't have to deal with these same complaints over and over!"

"I wish I could volunteer less time without stressing that things will explode in my face!"

If any of these thoughts came across your mind, you are not alone. Most condo board members share your frustration— and a genuine desire to make things better.

My goal in writing this book was to cover the basic challenges that every board deals with.

Such a brief overview, unfortunately, can't cover the detailed business processes and training required to *actually* turn your condominium into a smooth running and efficient corporation.

So I'd like to invite you to the next level.

I have created a video presentation that will show you how to solve the problems you deal with on a regular basis, once and for all. After you watch this presentation, you'll see how easy it is to improve communication, collaboration, access to information, keep owners informed, get repairs completed on time, and stop wasting your time in board meetings that only end in frustration.

If you are ready to a create a new level of efficiency that will protect the value of everyone's investment and make you a happy board member, then there is only one thing left to do.

WATCH THE VIDEO!

All you have to do is grab your computer or a smart phone and go to the website address below.

www.CondoBoardBook.com/video

If you truly want to get rid of all these problems once and for all I promise you this will be the best video presentation you'll watch this year.

See you in the video!

PS. Don't Waste Time and Go To
www.CondoBoardBook.com/video
Right Now!

BONUS

ASK THE EXPERTS ON THE CONDO WEB SHOW

Are you looking for more answers?

This book wasn't meant to answer every possible condo question or address every concern; otherwise it would turn into an encyclopedia and it would never get finished.

However, while writing this book an idea was born to address this issue. A live online TV show for condominiums — **The Condo Web Show**.

The Condo Web Show is a resource for all condo owners, residents, managers, and industry professionals where industry experts answer your questions and provide valuable education and information.

My goal is to help boards and managers improve the condominium industry. Not only through improve communication, collaboration, and access to information, but also through education and advice to those in need.

This is why **The Condo Web Show** has been created. So you can get your condominium questions answered by industry experts.

Don't miss this opportunity to get expert advice and guidance without any expensive consulting fees.

Go to the website below **RIGHT NOW** while it's still on your mind and subscribe so you never miss an upcoming episode!

www.CondoWebShow.com

Looking forward to speaking with you live!

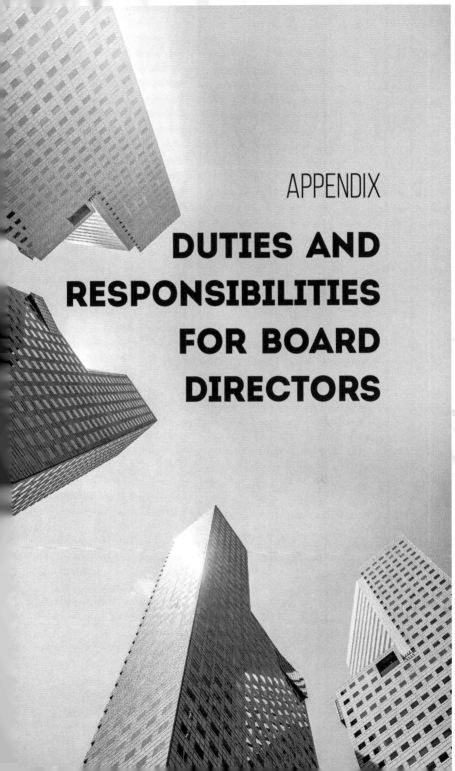

APPENDIX

DUTIES AND RESPONSIBILITIES FOR BOARD DIRECTORS

PRESIDENT

In general, the President supervises the business and affairs of a condo corporation. A great president will be one that is forward thinking, develops policies and procedures, communicates with the owners and residents, is faithful to the corporation, familiar and comfortable with the condo act, bylaws, rules and regulations, and is not afraid to implement new ideas and solutions that will benefit the board, owners, and the corporation.

A president should also have a good understanding of business concepts and procedures, laws, as well as accounting principles and budget planning. He or she should be a leader that supports and motivates the rest of the board.

- ✔ Ensures that the condominium act, regulations, bylaws, and policies are being followed and enforced
- ✔ Ensures that day to day operations are handled properly
- ✔ Monitors and reviews monthly and annual finances of the corporation
- ✔ Reviews annual service contracts with service providers as well as their licenses and insurance
- ✔ Reviews all submitted tenders
- ✔ Reviews and monitors work before payment is issued to service providers
- ✔ Provides direction and assistance to board members
- ✔ Schedules board meetings and set agendas
- ✔ Delegates responsibilities to appropriate persons

- ✔ Ensures board members are fulfilling their duties and responsibilities
- ✔ Ensures that business is conducted in a professional manner
- ✔ Ensures that all concerns are addressed and resolved
- ✔ Chairs board meetings and Annual General Meeting, unless a Chairperson is designated at the beginning of the meeting
- ✔ Ensures minutes and communication with owners is accurate
- ✔ Responds to inquiries
- ✔ Oversees managers' duties and activities

VICE-PRESIDENT

The Vice-President may share some of the duties of the President and distribute the workload fairly.

- ✔ Same responsibilities as the President, plus assists the president when required
- ✔ In the absence of the President, assumes the position of the President and chair meetings and/or general meetings

TREASURER

The Treasurer is responsible for the finances of the condo. The Treasurer ensures that the financial statements are accurate, the budget is completed in a timely fashion, the reserve fund is sufficient, invoices are reviewed and verified, and bills are paid. The treasurer should be someone that has a good understanding of accounting principles and budget planning with good organizational and planning skills.

- ✔ Maintains a ledger on fee status of each unit and provides unit account information when requested by owners
- ✔ Issues payments for services
- ✔ Maintains records of payments and collections
- ✔ Collects and deposits contributions and other monies payable to the Corporation
- ✔ Creates a monthly financial report
- ✔ Assists accountants or auditors in providing financial information for audits
- ✔ Issues fee arrears letters
- ✔ Responsible for Corporation's banking, at the direction of the board
- ✔ Ensures services have been provided before issuing payment
- ✔ Prepares draft budget
- ✔ Presents budget and/or audited statement to owners at the Annual General Meeting
- ✔ Provide investment options to the board.
- ✔ Performs other duties as required

SECRETARY

The secretary is a custodian of all the Corporation's records and communications with the owners and the board. The secretary should also have good computer skills as well as good verbal and written communication skills.

- ✔ Records and transcribes minutes of all board and General meetings
- ✔ Books meeting rooms or facilities when required
- ✔ Sends meeting notices
- ✔ Maintains an up to date list of owners
- ✔ Maintains the Corporation's records and documents such as licenses, insurance policies, tenders, contracts, etc.
- ✔ Creates and distributes newsletters, news announcements, and documents to owners and residents
- ✔ Responds to correspondence involving the Corporation as advised by the board
- ✔ Maintains a record of all received complaints and concerns from owners to be presented to the board

CHAIRPERSON

The Chairperson, whether it is the President, Vice-President or a designated person, is responsible for ensuring that the board meeting runs smoothly, on time, and on agenda. It is the chairperson that makes sure the discussions stay constructive, on topic and for the benefit of the corporation.

BEFORE YOU START
READING DOWNLOAD
YOUR TOOKLIT FOR <u>FREE</u>!

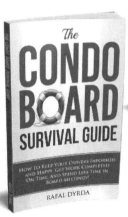

READ THIS FIRST

Just to say thanks for reading my book, I would like to give you a few bonuses to help you on your journey!

Download your **Condo Board Survival Toolkit** by visiting the website below:

www.CondoBoardBook.com/toolkit

Register your book & get your FREE bonuses